chapter 1: Intro

- Book Introduction

chapter 2: Introduction to Cybersecurity Scripts with Golang

- Brief overview of the importance of scripting in cybersecurity
- Introduction to the Go programming language and its benefits in security scripting
- Overview of the e-book's content

chapter 3: Setting Up Your Environment

- Installing Go on your system
- Setting up your development environment
- Configuring Go workspace

chapter 4: Basic Script Structure in Golang

- Explanation of Go's basic structure: packages, imports, and main function
- Creating your first Golang script: Hello World

chapter 5: Network Scanning with Golang

- Overview of network scanning in cybersecurity
- Building a basic network scanner using Golang
- Code snippet: Network scanner example

chapter 6: Web Application Security

- Introduction to web application security
- Building a simple URL crawler using Golang
- Code snippet: URL crawler example

chapter 7: Password Cracking Tools

- Overview of password cracking in cybersecurity
- Creating a password cracking tool using Golang
- Code snippet: Password cracking tool example

chapter 8: Encryption and Decryption Scripts

- Explanation of encryption and decryption in cybersecurity

- Developing a file encryption and decryption script with Golang
- Code snippet: Encryption and decryption example

chapter 9: File Integrity Checking

- Importance of file integrity checking in security
- Building a script to calculate and verify file hashes with Golang
- Code snippet: File hash verification example

chapter 10: Secure Data Transmission

- Exploring secure data transmission techniques
- Developing a basic secure chat application using Golang
- Code snippet: Secure chat application example

chapter 11: Log Analysis Scripts

- Overview of log analysis in cybersecurity
- Building a log parser to extract relevant information from log files using Golang
- Code snippet: Log parser example

chapter 12: Malware Analysis Tools

- Introduction to malware analysis
- Creating a basic script to analyze malware behavior using Golang
- Code snippet: Malware analysis script example

chapter 13: DDoS Mitigation Scripts

- Understanding DDoS attacks and mitigation
- Developing a simple DDoS mitigation script using Golang
- Code snippet: DDoS mitigation script example

chapter 14: Vulnerability Assessment Scripts

- Overview of vulnerability assessment in cybersecurity
- Building a basic vulnerability scanner using Golang
- Code snippet: Vulnerability scanner example

chapter 15: Security Automation with Golang

- Exploring the role of automation in cybersecurity
- Developing scripts to automate security tasks using Golang
- Code snippet: Security automation example

chapter 16: Secure Coding Practices

- Best practices for writing secure Golang scripts
- Handling user input securely
- Avoiding common vulnerabilities in your code

chapter 17: Testing and Debugging Security Scripts

- Importance of testing and debugging in security scripting
- Strategies for testing and debugging Golang security scripts

chapter 18: Continuous Learning and Resources

- Recommendations for further learning in Golang and cybersecurity
- Online resources, communities, and forums for Golang and security enthusiasts

chapter 19: Conclusion

- Recap of key points covered in the e-book
- Encouragement for readers to apply the knowledge gained and explore further

Introduction:

In an age where digital threats continue to evolve, the role of scripting in cybersecurity has become more critical than ever. This e-book is your comprehensive guide to leveraging the power of the Go programming language (Golang) to create effective cybersecurity scripts. As you navigate through these chapters, you'll discover how Golang's simplicity, speed, and robustness make it an ideal choice for developing security tools that help you defend against cyber threats.

Why Golang for Cybersecurity Scripts?

Golang, known for its efficiency and concise syntax, has gained popularity across various domains, including cybersecurity. With its native support for concurrency and cross-platform compilation, Golang empowers you to develop efficient and highly performant scripts tailored to your security needs.

What to Expect from This E-Book:

In the chapters that follow, you'll embark on a journey that takes you from the basics of setting up your Golang environment to creating practical cybersecurity scripts. You'll delve into network scanning, web application security, password cracking, encryption, and more. Each topic is accompanied by real code snippet examples that demonstrate how to put theory into practice.

By the end of this e-book, you'll have a toolkit of Golang scripts at your disposal, enabling you to enhance your organization's cybersecurity posture and effectively tackle emerging threats.

Who Should Read This E-Book?

Whether you're an aspiring cybersecurity professional, a developer seeking to expand your skill set, or an experienced practitioner looking to incorporate Golang into your security arsenal, this e-book is designed to cater to a wide range of audiences. No matter your background, a passion for both cybersecurity and programming will fuel your journey through these chapters.

Let's Begin the Journey:

Without further ado, let's dive into the world of cybersecurity scripts with Golang. We'll start by setting up your development environment so that you're ready to write your first lines of code. As we progress through the e-book, you'll gain valuable insights into various cybersecurity topics and learn how Golang can be harnessed to address them.

The world of cybersecurity is ever-evolving, and being armed with the ability to develop custom scripts is a formidable advantage. So, let's embark on this learning adventure and equip ourselves with the skills to secure our digital domains.

chapter 3: Setting Up Your Environment

Before you dive into creating cybersecurity scripts with Golang, it's essential to set up your development environment. This chapter will guide you through the process of installing Golang and configuring your workspace, ensuring you're ready to start writing code.

Installing Go:

1. Visit the official Golang website: https://golang.org/
2. Download the appropriate installer for your operating system (Windows, macOS, or Linux).
3. Follow the installation instructions for your platform.

Configuring Your Workspace:

After installing Go, it's time to set up your workspace. Go uses a specific directory structure known as the "workspace," which contains three main directories: `src`, `pkg`, and `bin`.

1. Create a directory to serve as your workspace. For example, you can create a directory called `go-workspace` in your home directory.
2. Inside your workspace directory, create the `src`, `pkg`, and `bin` directories. These directories will store your source code, package files, and compiled binaries, respectively.
3. Set the `GOPATH` environment variable to point to your workspace directory. This can typically be done by adding the following line to your shell configuration file (e.g., `.bashrc`, `.bash_profile`, or `.zshrc`):

    export GOPATH=/path/to/your/go-workspace

Verifying Your Installation:

To ensure that Golang is installed correctly and your workspace is set up properly, follow these steps:

1. Open a terminal or command prompt.
2. Run the following command to verify the Go installation:

    go version

3. You should see the installed Go version displayed in the output.

Creating Your First Golang Script: Hello World

Now that your environment is set up, let's create your first Golang script to print "Hello, World!" to the console.

1. Create a new directory for your script within the `src` directory of your workspace.
2. Inside this directory, create a new file named `hello.go`.
3. Open `hello.go` in a text editor and add the following code:

```go
package main

import "fmt"

func main() {
    fmt.Println("Hello, World!")
}
```

4. Save the file and return to your terminal.
5. Navigate to the directory containing `hello.go` and run the script using the following command:

```
go run hello.go
```

6. You should see the output: "Hello, World!"

With your environment set up and your first Golang script successfully running, you're ready to explore cybersecurity scripting using Golang in the upcoming chapters.

chapter 4: Basic Script Structure in Golang

Now that you have your development environment set up, it's time to dive deeper into the structure of a Golang script. In this section, we'll explore the fundamental components of a Golang script and create a basic script to solidify your understanding.

Understanding the Basic Structure:

A Golang script consists of several key components:

- **Package Declaration:** Every Go file belongs to a package. The package declaration at the beginning of the file indicates which package the code belongs to. For executable scripts, the package name should be `main`.

- **Imports:** Golang provides various built-in packages and libraries that you can use in your script. Import statements allow you to use functions and types from these packages.

- **Main Function:** The `main` function serves as the entry point of your script. When you run your script, the code inside the `main` function is executed.

Creating Your First Golang Script: Hello GoScript

Let's create a simple Golang script that goes beyond printing "Hello, World!" and showcases the basic script structure.

1. Create a new directory for your script within the `src` directory of your workspace.
2. Inside this directory, create a new file named `hellogoscript.go`.
3. Open `hellogoscript.go` in a text editor and add the following code:

```go
package main

import (
    "fmt"
    "os"
)

func main() {
    fmt.Println("Welcome to GoScript!")
    fmt.Println("This script takes command-line arguments.")

    // Fetch command-line arguments
    args := os.Args[1:]
    fmt.Println("Arguments:", args)
}
```

4. Save the file and return to your terminal.
5. Navigate to the directory containing `hellogoscript.go` and run the script using the following command:

```
go run hellogoscript.go arg1 arg2
```

6. Replace `arg1` and `arg2` with any arguments you'd like to pass to the script.

Exploring the Output:

- The script greets you with a welcome message.
- It informs you that it takes command-line arguments.
- It then fetches the command-line arguments you provided and displays them.

With this basic understanding of the structure of a Golang script, you're well-equipped to explore more complex topics, including building cybersecurity scripts. In the upcoming chapters, we'll delve into practical examples of security scripts using Golang.

chapter 5: Network Scanning with Golang

Network scanning is a crucial aspect of cybersecurity that helps identify potential vulnerabilities in a system. Golang's concurrency and network libraries make it well-suited for building efficient network scanning scripts. In this section, we'll explore how to create a basic network scanner using Golang.

Understanding Network Scanning:

Network scanning involves probing a network to discover active hosts, open ports, and potential vulnerabilities. It's an essential practice to ensure that your network is secure and free from unauthorized access points.

Building a Basic Network Scanner:

Let's create a simple network scanner that performs a **TCP port scan** on a specified target host.

1. Create a new directory for your network scanner script within the `src` directory of your workspace.
2. Inside this directory, create a new file named `networkscanner.go`.
3. Open `networkscanner.go` in a text editor and add the following code:

```go
package main

import (
    "fmt"
    "net"
    "strconv"
    "time"
)

func scanPort(target string, port int) {
    targetAddr := fmt.Sprintf("%s:%d", target, port)
    conn, err := net.DialTimeout("tcp", targetAddr, time.Second)
    if err == nil {
        conn.Close()
        fmt.Printf("Port %d: Open\n", port)
    }
```

```go
}

func main() {
    target := "localhost"
    ports := []int{80, 443, 22, 3306, 8080}

    fmt.Printf("Scanning ports on %s...\n", target)
    for _, port := range ports {
        go scanPort(target, port)
    }

    // Wait for all goroutines to finish
    time.Sleep(2 * time.Second)
}
```

4. Save the file and return to your terminal.
5. Navigate to the directory containing `networkscanner.go` and run the script using the following command:

```
go run networkscanner.go
```

6. The script will scan the specified ports on the target host (in this case, `localhost`) and display the results.

Exploring the Output:

- **The script defines a `scanPort` function** that attempts to establish a TCP connection to the target host on a specific port.
- **The `main` function** initiates the port scanning process by launching concurrent goroutines to scan each port in the `ports` slice.
- **After scanning,** the script waits for all the goroutines to finish before exiting.

This basic network scanner demonstrates how Golang's concurrency capabilities can be leveraged to efficiently perform network scanning tasks. In the upcoming chapters, we'll explore more cybersecurity scenarios and create corresponding Golang scripts.

chapter 6: Web Application Security

Web applications are often vulnerable to a range of security threats, making it crucial to regularly assess and secure them. Golang's web-related packages and capabilities enable the creation of tools for web application security testing. In this section, we'll explore how to build a simple URL crawler using Golang.

Importance of Web Application Security:

Web applications are common targets for various attacks, including cross-site scripting (XSS), SQL injection, and more. Performing security assessments and tests on web applications is essential to identify and mitigate vulnerabilities.

Creating a URL Crawler with Golang:

Let's create a basic URL crawler that visits a web chapter, extracts URLs from it, and adds them to a queue for further analysis.

1. Create a new directory for your URL crawler script within the `src` directory of your workspace.
2. Inside this directory, create a new file named `urlcrawler.go`.
3. Open `urlcrawler.go` in a text editor and add the following code:

```go
package main

import (
    "fmt"
    "net/http"
    "golang.org/x/net/html"
)

func crawlURL(url string, queue chan string) {
    resp, err := http.Get(url)
    if err != nil {
        return
    }
    defer resp.Body.Close()

    tokens := html.NewTokenizer(resp.Body)
    for {
        tokenType := tokens.Next()
        switch tokenType {
        case html.ErrorToken:
            return
        case html.StartTagToken, html.SelfClosingTagToken:
            token := tokens.Token()
            if token.Data == "a" {
                for _, attr := range token.Attr {
                    if attr.Key == "href" {
                        queue <- attr.Val
```

```go
                }
            }
        }
    }
}

func main() {
    startURL := "https://example.com"
    maxDepth := 2

    visited := make(map[string]bool)
    queue := make(chan string)

    go func() {
        queue <- startURL
    }()

    for url := range queue {
        if visited[url] {
            continue
        }

        fmt.Println("Visiting:", url)
        visited[url] = true

        go crawlURL(url, queue)

        if maxDepth > 0 {
            maxDepth--
            if maxDepth == 0 {
                close(queue)
            }
        }
    }
}
```

4. Save the file and return to your terminal.
5. Navigate to the directory containing `urlcrawler.go` and run the script using the following command:

```
go run urlcrawler.go
```

6. The script will start from the specified URL (`startURL`), crawl the web chapters, and display the visited URLs.

Exploring the Output:

- **The script defines a `crawlURL` function** that fetches a web chapter, extracts URLs from its anchor tags (`<a>`), and adds them to the queue for further crawling.
- **The `main` function** initiates the URL crawling process by launching a goroutine that adds the start URL to the queue.
- **The script keeps track of visited URLs** using the `visited` map and limits the crawling depth using the `maxDepth` variable.

This URL crawler provides a foundation for more advanced web application security tools. By extending this script, you can perform various tests and analyses on web applications to ensure their security.

In the subsequent chapters, we'll explore more scenarios and examples of cybersecurity scripts using Golang.

chapter 7: Password Cracking Tools

Password cracking is a vital aspect of cybersecurity, helping organizations assess the strength of their users' passwords and the effectiveness of their security measures. Golang's versatility allows us to build password cracking tools for various scenarios. In this section, we'll create a simple password cracking tool using Golang.

Understanding Password Cracking:

Password cracking involves attempting to discover passwords by systematically testing a list of possible passwords or using techniques like dictionary attacks and brute force attacks.

Creating a Password Cracking Tool:

Let's build a basic password cracking tool that performs a dictionary attack on a list of passwords.

1. Create a new directory for your password cracking script within the `src` directory of your workspace.
2. Inside this directory, create a new file named `passwordcracker.go`.
3. Open `passwordcracker.go` in a text editor and add the following code:

```go
package main
```

```go
import (
    "fmt"
    "io/ioutil"
    "strings"
)

func crackPassword(passwords []string, targetHash string) {
    for _, password := range passwords {
        hashed := hashFunction(password) // Replace with actual hash function
        if hashed == targetHash {
            fmt.Println("Password cracked:", password)
            return
        }
    }
    fmt.Println("Password not found in the dictionary.")
}

func hashFunction(input string) string {
    // Replace with the actual hash function you're targeting
    // For demonstration purposes, a simple hashing function is used here
    return input
}

func main() {
    targetHash := "5f4dcc3b5aa765d61d8327deb882cf99" // MD5 hash of "password"
    passwordFile := "passwords.txt"

    data, err := ioutil.ReadFile(passwordFile)
    if err != nil {
        fmt.Println("Error reading password file:", err)
        return
    }

    passwords := strings.Split(string(data), "\n")
    crackPassword(passwords, targetHash)
}
```

4. Save the file and return to your terminal.
5. Create a file named `passwords.txt` in the same directory and add a list of passwords, each on a new line.
6. Navigate to the directory containing `passwordcracker.go` and run the script using the following command:

go run passwordcracker.go

7. The script will attempt to crack the password hash by comparing it with hashes generated from the passwords in the `passwords.txt` file.

Exploring the Output:

- The script defines a `crackPassword` function that takes a list of passwords and a target hash as inputs. It iterates through the list and checks if the hash of each password matches the target hash.
- The `hashFunction` function simulates the hash function used in the actual system.
- The `main` function reads passwords from the `passwords.txt` file, calls the `crackPassword` function, and outputs the result.

This basic password cracking tool demonstrates how Golang can be employed to develop security-related scripts. In upcoming chapters, we'll continue exploring various cybersecurity scenarios and creating corresponding Golang scripts.

chapter 8: Encryption and Decryption Scripts

Encryption is a cornerstone of cybersecurity, ensuring the confidentiality of sensitive data. Golang's cryptographic packages make it suitable for building encryption and decryption scripts. In this section, we'll develop a simple file encryption and decryption script using Golang.

Understanding Encryption and Decryption:

Encryption involves converting data into an unreadable format using a key or algorithm. Decryption reverses this process, converting the encrypted data back to its original form.

Building a File Encryption and Decryption Script:

Let's create a basic script that encrypts a file using a symmetric encryption algorithm and then decrypts it back to its original form.

1. Create a new directory for your encryption and decryption script within the `src` directory of your workspace.
2. Inside this directory, create a new file named `encryption.go`.
3. Open `encryption.go` in a text editor and add the following code:

```go
package main

import (
```

```go
	"fmt"
	"io"
	"os"
	"crypto/aes"
	"crypto/cipher"
	"crypto/rand"
	"io/ioutil"
)

func encryptFile(inputFile, outputFile string, key []byte) error {
	plaintext, err := ioutil.ReadFile(inputFile)
	if err != nil {
		return err
	}

	block, err := aes.NewCipher(key)
	if err != nil {
		return err
	}

	ciphertext := make([]byte, aes.BlockSize+len(plaintext))
	iv := ciphertext[:aes.BlockSize]
	if _, err := io.ReadFull(rand.Reader, iv); err != nil {
		return err
	}

	stream := cipher.NewCTR(block, iv)
	stream.XORKeyStream(ciphertext[aes.BlockSize:], plaintext)

	return ioutil.WriteFile(outputFile, ciphertext, 0644)
}

func decryptFile(inputFile, outputFile string, key []byte) error {
	ciphertext, err := ioutil.ReadFile(inputFile)
	if err != nil {
		return err
	}

	block, err := aes.NewCipher(key)
	if err != nil {
		return err
	}

	iv := ciphertext[:aes.BlockSize]
```

```go
    ciphertext = ciphertext[aes.BlockSize:]

    stream := cipher.NewCTR(block, iv)
    stream.XORKeyStream(ciphertext, ciphertext)

    return ioutil.WriteFile(outputFile, ciphertext, 0644)
}

func main() {
    inputFile := "input.txt"
    encryptedFile := "encrypted.enc"
    decryptedFile := "decrypted.txt"
    key := []byte("supersecretpass")

    err := encryptFile(inputFile, encryptedFile, key)
    if err != nil {
        fmt.Println("Encryption error:", err)
        return
    }

    fmt.Println("File encrypted successfully.")

    err = decryptFile(encryptedFile, decryptedFile, key)
    if err != nil {
        fmt.Println("Decryption error:", err)
        return
    }

    fmt.Println("File decrypted successfully.")
}
```

4. Save the file and return to your terminal.
5. Create a file named `input.txt` in the same directory and add some text.
6. Navigate to the directory containing `encryption.go` and run the script using the following command:

```
go run encryption.go
```

7. The script will encrypt the contents of `input.txt`, save it as `encrypted.enc`, and then decrypt it back to `decrypted.txt`.

Exploring the Output:

- The script defines `encryptFile` and `decryptFile` functions that use the AES-CTR encryption mode for symmetric encryption and decryption.
- The `main` function demonstrates the encryption and decryption process by encrypting and then decrypting a file using a specified key.

This basic encryption and decryption script showcases Golang's cryptographic capabilities. In upcoming chapters, we'll continue exploring various cybersecurity scenarios and creating corresponding Golang scripts.

chapter 9: File Integrity Checking

Ensuring the integrity of files is a critical aspect of cybersecurity. File integrity checking helps detect unauthorized changes or tampering with files. Golang's hashing functions and file manipulation capabilities make it suitable for building file integrity checking scripts. In this section, we'll develop a script to calculate and verify file hashes using Golang.

Importance of File Integrity Checking:

File integrity checking involves generating a hash (checksum) of a file and comparing it with a previously calculated hash to determine if the file has been altered.

Building a File Integrity Checking Script:

Let's create a simple script that calculates and verifies the hash of a file to ensure its integrity.

1. Create a new directory for your file integrity checking script within the `src` directory of your workspace.
2. Inside this directory, create a new file named `fileintegrity.go`.
3. Open `fileintegrity.go` in a text editor and add the following code:

```go
package main

import (
    "fmt"
    "io"
    "os"
    "crypto/md5"
    "encoding/hex"
)

func calculateFileHash(filePath string) (string, error) {
    file, err := os.Open(filePath)
    if err != nil {
```

```go
        return "", err
    }
    defer file.Close()

    hash := md5.New()
    if _, err := io.Copy(hash, file); err != nil {
        return "", err
    }

    return hex.EncodeToString(hash.Sum(nil)), nil
}

func main() {
    filePath := "file.txt"
    expectedHash := "a94a8fe5ccb19ba61c4c0873d391e987982fbbd3"

    calculatedHash, err := calculateFileHash(filePath)
    if err != nil {
        fmt.Println("Error calculating hash:", err)
        return
    }

    if calculatedHash == expectedHash {
        fmt.Println("File integrity verified: Hash matches.")
    } else {
        fmt.Println("File integrity compromised: Hash does not match.")
    }
}
```

4. Save the file and return to your terminal.
5. Create a file named `file.txt` in the same directory and add some text.
6. Navigate to the directory containing `fileintegrity.go` and run the script using the following command:

```
go run fileintegrity.go
```

7. The script will calculate the hash of `file.txt` and compare it to the expected hash.

Exploring the Output:

- **The script defines a `calculateFileHash` function** that calculates the **MD5 hash** of a file using the `**crypto/md5**` **package.**

- The `main` function calculates the hash of the specified file and compares it to an expected hash value to verify the file's integrity.

This basic file integrity checking script demonstrates how Golang can be utilized to ensure the integrity of files. In upcoming chapters, we'll continue exploring various cybersecurity scenarios and creating corresponding Golang scripts.

chapter 10: Secure Data Transmission

Securing data transmission is paramount in the world of cybersecurity, especially when sensitive information needs to be exchanged between parties. Golang's networking capabilities enable the creation of secure communication channels. In this section, we'll develop a basic secure chat application using Golang.

Importance of Secure Data Transmission:

Secure data transmission ensures that information remains confidential and protected from interception or tampering during transit.

Building a Secure Chat Application:

Let's create a simple script that establishes a secure connection between a client and a server, allowing them to exchange encrypted messages.

1. Create a new directory for your secure chat application within the `src` directory of your workspace.
2. Inside this directory, create two files named `server.go` and `client.go`.
3. Open `server.go` in a text editor and add the following code:

```go
package main

import (
    "fmt"
    "net"
    "crypto/tls"
    "io"
)

func handleClient(conn net.Conn) {
    defer conn.Close()

    for {
        message := make([]byte, 1024)
```

```go
        _, err := conn.Read(message)
        if err != nil {
            return
        }
        fmt.Printf("Received: %s", message)
    }
}

func main() {
    cert, err := tls.LoadX509KeyPair("server.crt", "server.key")
    if err != nil {
        fmt.Println("Error loading certificates:", err)
        return
    }

    config := tls.Config{Certificates: []tls.Certificate{cert}}
    listener, err := tls.Listen("tcp", ":8080", &config)
    if err != nil {
        fmt.Println("Error creating listener:", err)
        return
    }

    fmt.Println("Server is listening on port 8080...")
    for {
        conn, err := listener.Accept()
        if err != nil {
            fmt.Println("Error accepting connection:", err)
            continue
        }
        go handleClient(conn)
    }
}
```

4. Open `client.go` in a text editor and add the following code:

```go
package main

import (
    "fmt"
    "net"
    "crypto/tls"
    "os"
```

```go
)

func main() {
    config := &tls.Config{InsecureSkipVerify: true}
    conn, err := tls.Dial("tcp", "localhost:8080", config)
    if err != nil {
        fmt.Println("Error connecting to server:", err)
        return
    }
    defer conn.Close()

    for {
        fmt.Print("Enter message: ")
        message := make([]byte, 1024)
        _, err := os.Stdin.Read(message)
        if err != nil {
            fmt.Println("Error reading input:", err)
            return
        }

        _, err = conn.Write(message)
        if err != nil {
            fmt.Println("Error sending message:", err)
            return
        }
    }
}
```

5. Save the files and return to your terminal.
6. Generate self-signed certificates for the server using the `openssl` command:

   openssl req -x509 -nodes -days 365 -newkey rsa:2048 -keyout server.key -out server.crt

7. Navigate to the directory containing the files and run the server using the following command:

   go run server.go

8. Open a new terminal window and navigate to the same directory. Run the client using the following command:

   go run client.go

9. Enter messages in the client terminal, and they will be securely transmitted to the server.

Exploring the Output:

- **The `server.go` script creates a TLS-enabled server** that listens for incoming connections and handles incoming messages.
- **The `client.go` script establishes a secure connection to the server** and allows the user to send encrypted messages.

This basic secure chat application showcases Golang's ability to create secure communication channels. In upcoming chapters, we'll continue exploring various cybersecurity scenarios and creating corresponding Golang scripts.

chapter 11: Automating Security Tasks

Automation plays a crucial role in cybersecurity, allowing repetitive and time-consuming tasks to be performed efficiently and consistently. Golang's scripting capabilities can be harnessed to automate various security-related tasks. In this section, we'll create a simple script that automates the process of checking the security headers of a website.

Importance of Automation in Cybersecurity:

Automation enables security professionals to scale their efforts, perform routine tasks with accuracy, and respond quickly to emerging threats.

Automating Security Header Checks:

Let's build a script that automates the process of checking the security headers of a website to ensure it adheres to best practices.

1. Create a new directory for your security header check script within the `src` directory of your workspace.
2. Inside this directory, create a new file named `securityheaders.go`.
3. Open `securityheaders.go` in a text editor and add the following code:

```go
package main

import (
    "fmt"
    "net/http"
)

func checkSecurityHeaders(url string) {
    resp, err := http.Get(url)
```

```go
    if err != nil {
        fmt.Println("Error:", err)
        return
    }
    defer resp.Body.Close()

    securityHeaders := map[string]string{
        "Strict-Transport-Security":  "max-age=31536000",
        "Content-Security-Policy":    "default-src 'self'",
        "X-Frame-Options":            "DENY",
        "X-Content-Type-Options":     "nosniff",
        "X-XSS-Protection":           "1; mode=block",
    }

    fmt.Printf("Security headers for %s:\n", url)
    for header, expectedValue := range securityHeaders {
        value := resp.Header.Get(header)
        if value == expectedValue {
            fmt.Printf("%s: %s [OK]\n", header, value)
        } else {
            fmt.Printf("%s: %s [Mismatch: Expected %s]\n", header, value, expectedValue)
        }
    }
}

func main() {
    url := "https://example.com"
    checkSecurityHeaders(url)
}
```

4. Save the file and return to your terminal.
5. Navigate to the directory containing `securityheaders.go` and run the script using the following command:

```
go run securityheaders.go
```

6. The script will check the security headers of the specified URL and display the results.

Exploring the Output:

- The script defines a `checkSecurityHeaders` function that sends an HTTP request to a specified URL and checks for the presence of security headers.

- The function compares the actual header values with the expected values and provides feedback on whether they match.

This basic security header check script demonstrates how Golang can be employed to automate security-related tasks. In upcoming chapters, we'll continue exploring various cybersecurity scenarios and creating corresponding Golang scripts.

chapter 12: Log Analysis for Intrusion Detection

Log analysis is a critical component of cybersecurity, aiding in the detection of suspicious activities or unauthorized access attempts. Golang's capabilities can be utilized to build tools for parsing and analyzing log files. In this section, we'll develop a basic log analysis script using Golang.

Importance of Log Analysis in Cybersecurity:

Log analysis helps identify patterns, anomalies, and potential security breaches in system logs, leading to faster detection and response to security incidents.

Building a Log Analysis Script:

Let's create a simple script that parses log files, searches for specific patterns, and alerts the user if suspicious activities are detected.

1. Create a new directory for your log analysis script within the `src` directory of your workspace.
2. Inside this directory, create a new file named `loganalyzer.go`.
3. Open `loganalyzer.go` in a text editor and add the following code:

```go
package main

import (
    "fmt"
    "bufio"
    "os"
    "strings"
)

func analyzeLogFile(filePath string, keyword string) {
    file, err := os.Open(filePath)
    if err != nil {
        fmt.Println("Error opening file:", err)
        return
```

```go
	}
	defer file.Close()

	scanner := bufio.NewScanner(file)
	for scanner.Scan() {
		line := scanner.Text()
		if strings.Contains(line, keyword) {
			fmt.Println("Suspicious activity detected:")
			fmt.Println(line)
			fmt.Println("-----")
		}
	}

	if err := scanner.Err(); err != nil {
		fmt.Println("Error reading file:", err)
	}
}

func main() {
	logFile := "system.log"
	keyword := "Unauthorized access"
	analyzeLogFile(logFile, keyword)
}
```

4. Save the file and return to your terminal.
5. Create a file named `system.log` in the same directory and add some log entries, including the specified keyword (`Unauthorized access`).
6. Navigate to the directory containing `loganalyzer.go` and run the script using the following command:

```
go run loganalyzer.go
```

7. The script will analyze the log file for entries containing the specified keyword and display them.

Exploring the Output:

- The script defines an `analyzeLogFile` function that reads a log file line by line and searches for occurrences of the specified keyword.
- If a line containing the keyword is found, the script alerts the user by displaying the suspicious log entry.

This basic log analysis script demonstrates how Golang can be leveraged to automate the detection of suspicious activities in log files. In upcoming chapters, we'll continue exploring various cybersecurity scenarios and creating corresponding Golang scripts.

chapter 13: Vulnerability Scanning

Regularly scanning systems and applications for vulnerabilities is a crucial step in maintaining a strong cybersecurity posture. Golang's capabilities can be harnessed to build vulnerability scanning tools that identify potential security weaknesses. In this section, we'll develop a basic vulnerability scanning script using Golang.

Importance of Vulnerability Scanning in Cybersecurity:

Vulnerability scanning helps identify security flaws in software, systems, and networks, enabling organizations to patch and remediate vulnerabilities before they can be exploited.

Building a Vulnerability Scanning Script:

Let's create a simple script that performs a basic vulnerability scan by checking for open ports on a target host.

1. Create a new directory for your vulnerability scanning script within the `src` directory of your workspace.
2. Inside this directory, create a new file named `vulnscanner.go`.
3. Open `vulnscanner.go` in a text editor and add the following code:

```go
package main

import (
    "fmt"
    "net"
    "time"
)

func scanPort(target string, port int) {
    targetAddr := fmt.Sprintf("%s:%d", target, port)
    conn, err := net.DialTimeout("tcp", targetAddr, time.Second)
    if err == nil {
        conn.Close()
        fmt.Printf("Port %d: Open\n", port)
    }
}
```

```go
func main() {
    target := "example.com"
    ports := []int{80, 443, 22, 3306, 8080}

    fmt.Printf("Scanning ports on %s...\n", target)
    for _, port := range ports {
        go scanPort(target, port)
    }

    // Wait for all goroutines to finish
    time.Sleep(2 * time.Second)
}
```

4. Save the file and return to your terminal.
5. Navigate to the directory containing `vulnscanner.go` and run the script using the following command:

```
go run vulnscanner.go
```

6. The script will scan the specified ports on the target host (in this case, `example.com`) and display the results.

Exploring the Output:

- The script defines a `scanPort` function that attempts to establish a TCP connection to the target host on a specific port.
- The `main` function initiates the vulnerability scanning process by launching concurrent goroutines to scan each port in the `ports` slice.

This basic vulnerability scanning script demonstrates how Golang can be utilized to build tools for identifying potential security weaknesses. In upcoming chapters, we'll continue exploring various cybersecurity scenarios and creating corresponding Golang scripts.

chapter 14: Threat Intelligence Gathering

Staying informed about emerging threats and malicious activities is crucial in cybersecurity. Golang can be used to build tools that gather threat intelligence from various sources, helping organizations anticipate and mitigate potential risks. In this section, we'll develop a basic threat intelligence gathering script using Golang.

Importance of Threat Intelligence in Cybersecurity:

Threat intelligence provides valuable insights into the tactics, techniques, and procedures used by threat actors, enabling proactive defense and incident response strategies.

Building a Threat Intelligence Gathering Script:

Let's create a simple script that fetches and displays the latest threat intelligence indicators from a threat intelligence feed.

1. Create a new directory for your threat intelligence gathering script within the `src` directory of your workspace.
2. Inside this directory, create a new file named `threatintel.go`.
3. Open `threatintel.go` in a text editor and add the following code:

```go
package main

import (
    "fmt"
    "net/http"
    "encoding/json"
)

type ThreatIndicator struct {
    Type    string `json:"type"`
    Value   string `json:"value"`
    Source  string `json:"source"`
}

func fetchThreatIndicators(feedURL string) ([]ThreatIndicator, error) {
    response, err := http.Get(feedURL)
    if err != nil {
        return nil, err
    }
    defer response.Body.Close()

    var indicators []ThreatIndicator
    decoder := json.NewDecoder(response.Body)
    err = decoder.Decode(&indicators)
    if err != nil {
        return nil, err
    }

    return indicators, nil
}
```

```go
func main() {
    threatIntelFeed := "https://example.com/threatfeed"
    indicators, err := fetchThreatIndicators(threatIntelFeed)
    if err != nil {
        fmt.Println("Error fetching threat indicators:", err)
        return
    }

    fmt.Println("Latest Threat Indicators:")
    for _, indicator := range indicators {
        fmt.Printf("Type: %s, Value: %s, Source: %s\n", indicator.Type, indicator.Value,
indicator.Source)
    }
}
```

4. Save the file and return to your terminal.
5. Navigate to the directory containing `threatintel.go` and run the script using the following
command:

```
go run threatintel.go
```

6. The script will fetch the latest threat intelligence indicators from the specified feed and display
them.

Exploring the Output:

- **The script defines a `ThreatIndicator`** structure to represent threat intelligence indicators.
- **The `fetchThreatIndicators` function fetches threat indicators** from a specified feed URL
and decodes the JSON response.
- **The `main` function** fetches and displays the latest threat intelligence indicators.

This basic threat intelligence gathering script demonstrates how Golang can be employed to
fetch and process threat intelligence data. In upcoming chapters, we'll continue exploring
various cybersecurity scenarios and creating corresponding Golang scripts.

chapter 15: Password Management Tools

Effective password management is a cornerstone of cybersecurity. Golang can be used to
create tools that generate, store, and manage passwords securely. In this section, we'll develop
a basic password management tool using Golang.

Importance of Password Management in Cybersecurity:

Strong and unique passwords are essential to prevent unauthorized access and protect
sensitive information.

Building a Password Management Tool:

Let's create a simple script that generates strong random passwords and securely stores them
in a password vault.

1. Create a new directory for your password management tool within the `src` directory of your
workspace.
2. Inside this directory, create a new file named `passwordmanager.go`.
3. Open `passwordmanager.go` in a text editor and add the following code:

```go
package main

import (
    "fmt"
    "os"
    "io/ioutil"
    "crypto/rand"
    "encoding/base64"
)

const passwordVault = "passwords.txt"

func generateRandomPassword(length int) (string, error) {
    buffer := make([]byte, length)
    _, err := rand.Read(buffer)
    if err != nil {
        return "", err
    }
    return base64.StdEncoding.EncodeToString(buffer), nil
}

func savePassword(service, username, password string) error {
    entry := fmt.Sprintf("Service: %s\nUsername: %s\nPassword: %s\n\n", service, username,
password)
    return ioutil.WriteFile(passwordVault, []byte(entry), os.ModeAppend)
}

func main() {
```

```go
    service := "example.com"
    username := "user123"
    passwordLength := 12

    password, err := generateRandomPassword(passwordLength)
    if err != nil {
        fmt.Println("Error generating password:", err)
        return
    }

    err = savePassword(service, username, password)
    if err != nil {
        fmt.Println("Error saving password:", err)
        return
    }

    fmt.Println("Password generated and saved securely.")
}
```

4. Save the file and return to your terminal.
5. Navigate to the directory containing `passwordmanager.go` and run the script using the following command:

```
go run passwordmanager.go
```

6. The script will generate a strong random password, save it along with service details in the `passwords.txt` vault.

Exploring the Output:

- **The script defines a `generateRandomPassword` function** that generates a strong random password of a specified length.
- **The `savePassword` function** saves the service details, username, and password in the password vault file.
- **The `main` function** generates a random password and saves it securely in the password vault.

This basic password management tool demonstrates how Golang can be employed to generate and store strong passwords. In upcoming chapters, we'll continue exploring various cybersecurity scenarios and creating corresponding Golang scripts.

chapter 16: Network Traffic Analysis

Analyzing network traffic helps detect anomalies and potential security breaches. Golang can be utilized to build tools that capture and analyze network packets, providing insights into network activity. In this section, we'll develop a basic network traffic analysis tool using Golang.

Importance of Network Traffic Analysis in Cybersecurity:

Network traffic analysis helps identify unauthorized access, data exfiltration, and suspicious activities occurring within a network.

Building a Network Traffic Analysis Tool:

Let's create a simple script that captures and analyzes network packets using Golang's `github.com/google/gopacket` library.

1. Create a new directory for your network traffic analysis tool within the `src` directory of your workspace.
2. Inside this directory, create a new file named `networkanalyzer.go`.
3. Open `networkanalyzer.go` in a text editor and add the following code:

```go
package main

import (
    "fmt"
    "log"
    "github.com/google/gopacket"
    "github.com/google/gopacket/pcap"
)

func main() {
    device := "eth0"
    snapshotLen := 1024
    promiscuous := false
    timeout := pcap.BlockForever

    handle, err := pcap.OpenLive(device, int32(snapshotLen), promiscuous, timeout)
    if err != nil {
        log.Fatal(err)
    }
    defer handle.Close()

    packetSource := gopacket.NewPacketSource(handle, handle.LinkType())
```

```go
    for packet := range packetSource.Packets() {
        fmt.Println(packet)
    }
}
```

4. Save the file and return to your terminal.
5. Navigate to the directory containing `networkanalyzer.go` and run the script using the following command:

```
  go run networkanalyzer.go
```

6. The script will capture and display network packets from the specified network interface (`eth0`).

Exploring the Output:

- **The script uses the `github.com/google/gopacket` library** to capture and analyze network packets.
- **The `main` function** opens a live capture handle on the specified network interface and processes incoming packets.

This basic network traffic analysis tool demonstrates how Golang can be employed to capture and analyze network packets. In upcoming chapters, we'll continue exploring various cybersecurity scenarios and creating corresponding Golang scripts.

chapter 17: Secure API Development

Developing secure APIs is crucial for protecting data and ensuring that applications interact safely with each other. Golang's capabilities can be harnessed to build secure APIs that implement authentication and authorization mechanisms. In this section, we'll develop a basic secure API using Golang.

Importance of Secure API Development in Cybersecurity:

Secure APIs prevent unauthorized access to sensitive data and protect against attacks like injection and data exposure.

Building a Secure API:

Let's create a simple script that sets up a basic API server with authentication and authorization features.

1. Create a new directory for your secure API within the `src` directory of your workspace.
2. Inside this directory, create a new file named `secureapi.go`.
3. Open `secureapi.go` in a text editor and add the following code:

```go
package main

import (
    "fmt"
    "net/http"
    "github.com/gorilla/mux"
    "github.com/dgrijalva/jwt-go"
)

var secretKey = []byte("supersecretkey")

func handleAPIRequest(w http.ResponseWriter, r *http.Request) {
    w.Header().Set("Content-Type", "application/json")
    w.WriteHeader(http.StatusOK)
    fmt.Fprintf(w, `{"message": "Access granted to secure resource"}`)
}

func requireTokenAuthentication(next http.Handler) http.Handler {
    return http.HandlerFunc(func(w http.ResponseWriter, r *http.Request) {
        tokenString := r.Header.Get("Authorization")
        if tokenString == "" {
            w.WriteHeader(http.StatusUnauthorized)
            fmt.Fprintf(w, `{"error": "Missing authentication token"}`)
            return
        }

        token, err := jwt.Parse(tokenString, func(token *jwt.Token) (interface{}, error) {
            return secretKey, nil
        })

        if err != nil || !token.Valid {
            w.WriteHeader(http.StatusUnauthorized)
            fmt.Fprintf(w, `{"error": "Invalid authentication token"}`)
            return
        }

        next.ServeHTTP(w, r)
    })
}
```

```go
func main() {
    router := mux.NewRouter()
    router.HandleFunc("/api/secure", handleAPIRequest).Methods("GET")
    secureRouter := requireTokenAuthentication(router)

    http.Handle("/", secureRouter)
    fmt.Println("Secure API server is running on :8080...")
    http.ListenAndServe(":8080", nil)
}
```

4. Save the file and return to your terminal.
5. Navigate to the directory containing `secureapi.go` and run the script using the following command:

```
go run secureapi.go
```

6. The script will start a secure API server on port `8080`.

Exploring the Output:

- The script sets up a secure API server using the `github.com/gorilla/mux` router and the `github.com/dgrijalva/jwt-go` library for **JWT-based** authentication.

- The `requireTokenAuthentication` middleware ensures that only requests with valid JWT tokens can access the secure endpoint.

This basic secure API demonstrates how Golang can be employed to build APIs with authentication and authorization mechanisms. In upcoming chapters, we'll continue exploring various cybersecurity scenarios and creating corresponding Golang scripts.

chapter 18: Incident Response Automation

Automating incident response processes is crucial for swift and effective handling of security incidents. Golang's capabilities can be leveraged to build scripts that automate incident detection, alerting, and response actions. In this section, we'll develop a basic incident response automation script using Golang.

Importance of Incident Response Automation in Cybersecurity:

Automated incident response helps reduce response times, minimize damage, and ensure consistent actions during security incidents.

Building an Incident Response Automation Script:

Let's create a simple script that simulates incident detection, alerts, and response actions.

1. Create a new directory for your incident response automation script within the `src` directory of your workspace.
2. Inside this directory, create a new file named `incidentresponse.go`.
3. Open `incidentresponse.go` in a text editor and add the following code:

```go
package main

import (
    "fmt"
    "time"
)

func detectIncident() bool {
    // Simulate incident detection logic
    return true
}

func sendAlert(message string) {
    // Simulate sending alerts
    fmt.Printf("Alert sent: %s\n", message)
}

func performResponseActions() {
    // Simulate incident response actions
    fmt.Println("Performing incident response actions...")
    time.Sleep(3 * time.Second)
    fmt.Println("Incident response completed.")
}

func main() {
    if detectIncident() {
        incidentMessage := "Security breach detected!"
        sendAlert(incidentMessage)
        performResponseActions()
    } else {
        fmt.Println("No incidents detected.")
    }
}
```

4. Save the file and return to your terminal.
5. Navigate to the directory containing `incidentresponse.go` and run the script using the following command:

    go run incidentresponse.go

6. The script will simulate incident detection, alerting, and response actions.

Exploring the Output:

- **The script defines functions** for simulating incident detection, alerting, and response actions.
- **The `main` function** initiates the incident response automation process by calling the appropriate functions based on incident detection.

This basic incident response automation script demonstrates how Golang can be utilized to automate the handling of security incidents. In upcoming chapters, we'll continue exploring various cybersecurity scenarios and creating corresponding Golang scripts.

chapter 19: Security Policy Enforcement

Enforcing security policies is essential to maintain a consistent and secure environment. Golang's capabilities can be harnessed to build tools that enforce security policies across systems and applications. In this section, we'll develop a basic security policy enforcement script using Golang.

Importance of Security Policy Enforcement in Cybersecurity:

Security policies provide guidelines and rules that ensure compliance with security standards and protect against security threats.

Building a Security Policy Enforcement Script:

Let's create a simple script that enforces a security policy by checking whether a user's password meets the required complexity criteria.

1. Create a new directory for your security policy enforcement script within the `src` directory of your workspace.
2. Inside this directory, create a new file named `policyenforcer.go`.
3. Open `policyenforcer.go` in a text editor and add the following code:

```go
package main
```

```go
import (
	"fmt"
	"regexp"
)

const (
	minPasswordLength = 8
	minUppercaseChars = 1
	minLowercaseChars = 1
	minDigits         = 1
	minSpecialChars   = 1
)

func enforcePasswordPolicy(password string) bool {
	if len(password) < minPasswordLength {
		return false
	}

	uppercaseCount := 0
	lowercaseCount := 0
	digitCount := 0
	specialCharCount := 0

	for _, char := range password {
		if char >= 'A' && char <= 'Z' {
			uppercaseCount++
		} else if char >= 'a' && char <= 'z' {
			lowercaseCount++
		} else if char >= '0' && char <= '9' {
			digitCount++
		} else {
			specialCharCount++
		}
	}

	return uppercaseCount >= minUppercaseChars &&
		lowercaseCount >= minLowercaseChars &&
		digitCount >= minDigits &&
		specialCharCount >= minSpecialChars
}

func main() {
	userPassword := "SecurePass123!"
```

```go
    if enforcePasswordPolicy(userPassword) {
        fmt.Println("Password meets security policy.")
    } else {
        fmt.Println("Password does not meet security policy.")
    }
}
```

4. Save the file and return to your terminal.
5. Navigate to the directory containing `policyenforcer.go` and run the script using the following command:

```
go run policyenforcer.go
```

6. The script will check whether the specified password meets the security policy criteria.

Exploring the Output:

- **The script defines a `enforcePasswordPolicy` function** that enforces a password security policy based on length, uppercase, lowercase, digits, and special characters.
- **The `main` function** checks whether a user's password meets the security policy criteria.

This basic security policy enforcement script demonstrates how Golang can be employed to enforce security policies across user inputs. In upcoming chapters, we'll continue exploring various cybersecurity scenarios and creating corresponding Golang scripts.

chapter 20: Continuous Monitoring and Alerts

Continuous monitoring and real-time alerts are crucial for identifying and responding to security incidents promptly. Golang's capabilities can be harnessed to build tools that monitor system and application metrics and trigger alerts when anomalies are detected. In this final section, we'll develop a basic continuous monitoring and alerting script using Golang.

Importance of Continuous Monitoring and Alerts in Cybersecurity:

Continuous monitoring allows organizations to detect and respond to security threats as they arise, minimizing the impact of potential breaches.

Building a Continuous Monitoring and Alerting Script:

Let's create a simple script that simulates continuous monitoring of system metrics and triggers alerts for abnormal conditions.

1. Create a new directory for your monitoring and alerting script within the `src` directory of your workspace.
2. Inside this directory, create a new file named `monitoring.go`.
3. Open `monitoring.go` in a text editor and add the following code:

```go
package main

import (
    "fmt"
    "math/rand"
    "time"
)

const (
    normalThreshold  = 70
    alertThreshold   = 90
    checkInterval    = 5 * time.Second
    alertCheckPeriods = 3
)

func monitorSystemMetrics() {
    rand.Seed(time.Now().UnixNano())

    for {
        cpuUsage := rand.Intn(101)
        fmt.Printf("CPU Usage: %d%%\n", cpuUsage)

        if cpuUsage >= alertThreshold {
            fmt.Println("ALERT: High CPU usage detected!")
        }

        time.Sleep(checkInterval)
    }
}

func main() {
    fmt.Println("Starting continuous monitoring...")
    monitorSystemMetrics()
}
```

4. Save the file and return to your terminal.

5. Navigate to the directory containing `monitoring.go` and run the script using the following command:

    go run monitoring.go

6. The script will simulate continuous monitoring of system metrics (in this case, CPU usage) and trigger alerts for high usage.

Exploring the Output:

- **The script defines a `monitorSystemMetrics` function** that simulates monitoring system metrics (CPU usage) at regular intervals.
- If the CPU usage exceeds the defined alert threshold, an alert message is displayed.

This basic continuous monitoring and alerting script demonstrates how Golang can be employed to monitor system metrics and trigger alerts in real-time. With this, we conclude our exploration of cybersecurity scripts using Golang.

Thank you for joining us on this journey through various cybersecurity scenarios and their corresponding Golang scripts. The examples provided in this e-book serve as a starting point for building more comprehensive and robust tools to address the diverse challenges of cybersecurity. If you have any further questions or would like to delve deeper into any specific topic, feel free to reach out. Happy scripting and stay secure!

Conclusion and Next Steps

Congratulations! You've embarked on a journey through the world of cybersecurity scripting with Golang, exploring various scenarios and building practical solutions. Armed with this knowledge, you're better equipped to enhance security in your digital endeavors.

In this e-book, we covered a range of cybersecurity areas:

- Automating security header checks for web applications.
- Analyzing logs for intrusion detection and security incident monitoring.
- Conducting vulnerability scans to identify potential weaknesses.
- Gathering threat intelligence from external sources.
- Managing passwords securely.
- Analyzing network traffic for anomalies.
- Building secure APIs with authentication and authorization.
- Automating incident response to minimize damage.
- Enforcing security policies across systems and applications.
- Implementing continuous monitoring and real-time alerts.

These scripts serve as valuable starting points for your cybersecurity initiatives. However, the world of cybersecurity is vast and ever-evolving. Here are some next steps you can consider:

1. Customization: Tailor the provided scripts to your specific needs. Security is not one-size-fits-all, so adapt the scripts to match your organization's requirements.

2. Further Learning: Continue your learning journey by exploring advanced Golang concepts, cybersecurity frameworks, and industry best practices.

3. Integration: Integrate the scripts into your existing cybersecurity infrastructure. Automation and orchestration are key to effective cybersecurity.

4. Collaboration: Engage with the cybersecurity community to share knowledge and stay updated on the latest threats and solutions.

5. Stay Informed: Cyber threats evolve rapidly, so stay informed about emerging threats and vulnerabilities through threat intelligence feeds and cybersecurity news sources.

Remember that cybersecurity is an ongoing process, and your commitment to it is essential. With the power of Golang and your newfound scripting skills, you have the tools to bolster security, protect data, and respond effectively to the ever-changing threat landscape.

Thank you for joining us on this cybersecurity scripting journey. Stay secure, keep learning, and keep scripting!

If you have any questions or need further assistance, feel free to reach out. Happy scripting!

Disclaimer

The information provided in this e-book, "Cybersecurity Scripts with Golang: Practical Guide with Code Examples," is intended for educational and informational purposes only. The content presented here is based on knowledge available up to the date of this e-book's publication, which is [09/16/2023], and is subject to change.

The authors and the publisher of this e-book make no representations or warranties of any kind, express or implied, about the completeness, accuracy, reliability, suitability, or availability of the information, code snippets, or examples contained herein. Any reliance you place on such information is strictly at your own risk.

The content in this e-book does not constitute professional cybersecurity or legal advice. Cybersecurity is a complex field, and specific circumstances may require individualized solutions or legal consultation. Before implementing any security measures or scripts discussed in this e-book, you should consult with cybersecurity professionals or legal experts who can assess your unique situation and provide tailored recommendations.

The authors and the publisher disclaim any liability for any loss or damage, including without limitation, indirect or consequential loss or damage, or any loss or damage whatsoever arising from the use of this e-book or its content.

While every effort has been made to ensure that the information presented is accurate and up to date, the field of cybersecurity is constantly evolving, and new threats and vulnerabilities may emerge. Therefore, it is essential to stay informed about the latest developments and best practices in cybersecurity.

This e-book may contain references to third-party websites, products, or services. These references are provided for informational purposes only, and the authors and the publisher do not endorse or assume any responsibility for the content, functionality, or security of such third-party resources.

By using this e-book, you agree to the terms and conditions outlined in this disclaimer. If you do not agree with these terms, please discontinue using this e-book.

Please consult with qualified professionals and conduct thorough testing before implementing any security measures or scripts in your own environment. Your cybersecurity and legal compliance are your responsibility, and the authors and the publisher are not liable for any consequences resulting from your actions.

This disclaimer is subject to change without notice. For the most current version of the disclaimer, please refer to the publisher's website.

Thank You and Keep Striving!

Dear Reader,

As you reach the end of **"Cybersecurity Scripts with Golang: Practical Guide with Code Examples"** we want to extend our heartfelt thanks for joining us on this educational journey. Your commitment to learning and enhancing your cybersecurity skills is commendable.

Remember that knowledge is a powerful tool, but it is your determination, curiosity, and continuous effort that will set you on a path to success. The world of cybersecurity is ever-evolving, and there is always something new to discover, explore, and master.

Here's a motivational quote to inspire you on your journey:

**"Success is not final, failure is not fatal: It is the courage to continue that counts." —
Winston Churchill**

Embrace challenges as opportunities for growth, and never stop striving to learn, adapt, and be
better. Your dedication to cybersecurity not only enhances your own capabilities but also
contributes to a safer digital world for all.

We encourage you to keep learning, keep experimenting, and keep making a positive impact.
Your cybersecurity expertise has the potential to protect organizations, individuals, and valuable
data.

If you ever find yourself facing obstacles or uncertainties, remember that every cybersecurity
expert started as a learner. Your journey is unique, and your progress is a testament to your
dedication.

Once again, thank you for choosing **"Cybersecurity Scripts with Golang"** as your resource for
advancing your cybersecurity skills. We wish you continued success in your cybersecurity
endeavors and in all your future learning pursuits.

www.ingramcontent.com/pod-product-compliance
Lightning Source LLC
Chambersburg PA
CBHW080922260726

48661CB00009B/3776